EGG STORY

by ANCA HARITON

DUTTON CHILDREN'S BOOKS
NEW YORK

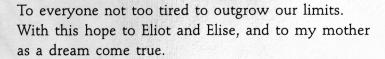

To everyone not too tired to outgrow our limits.
With this hope to Eliot and Elise, and to my mother
as a dream come true.

Published in the United States by
Dutton Children's Books,
a division of Penguin Books USA Inc.
375 Hudson Street, New York, New York 10014

Designer: Joseph Rutt

Printed in Hong Kong
First Edition   10 9 8 7 6 5 4 3 2 1

Library of Congress Cataloging-in-Publication Data

Hariton, Anca.
  Egg story/Anca Hariton.—1st ed.
    p. cm.
  Summary: Follows an egg from the time it is laid, through
its incubation under the hen's body, to the chick's birth after
twenty-one days.
  ISBN 0-525-44861-6
  1. Chickens—Embryos—Juvenile literature.   2. Eggs—Juvenile
literature.   3. Chicks—Juvenile literature.   [1. Chickens—Embryos.
2. Eggs.] I. Title.
QL959.H28   1992
598'.617—dc20   91-34588 CIP AC

"Cock-a-doodle-doo!"
The rooster crows and the farm wakes up.

The cat stretches, the dog yawns,
and the ducks flap their wings.

The gray hen cackles from the henhouse.

She has just laid an egg.

The outside of the egg
is smooth and seamless.

Inside the egg, on the yolk, there is a tiny white spot. If the egg is kept warm, a chick will grow from this spot. Everything the chick needs for growing until it is ready to hatch is inside the egg. The chick will hatch in about twenty-one days.

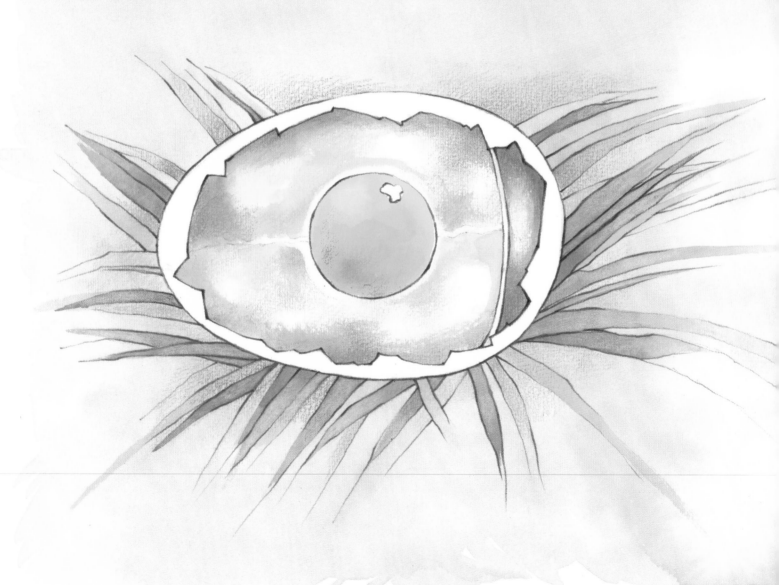

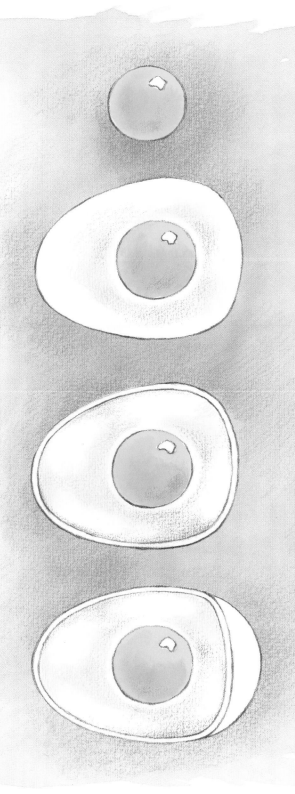

The yellow yolk, in the middle, provides food.

The chick will start to grow in the clear white that surrounds the yolk. It provides water and food, and it also acts as a cushion that keeps the tiny chick from bumping around.

A thin sac wraps around the white and the yolk. This sac sticks to the inside of the shell and almost fills the egg.

The small space that is left at the end of the egg is filled with air.

The gray hen lays more eggs, one at a time. She puffs out her feathers and sits quietly on the eggs. She keeps them warm all day.

She keeps them warm all night.

The tiny white spot in the egg gets bigger. It changes color and shape. At seven days old it starts to look a little like a chick.

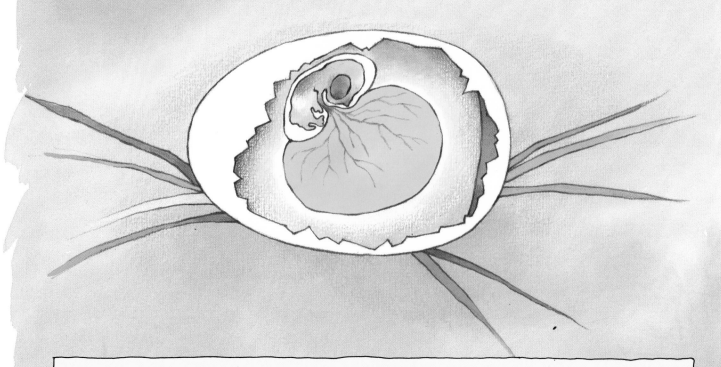

Compared with the rest of the body, the head and eyes are very big.

The chick's heart is already pumping. It pumps red blood through tiny tubes. The blood carries food from the yolk to the growing chick.

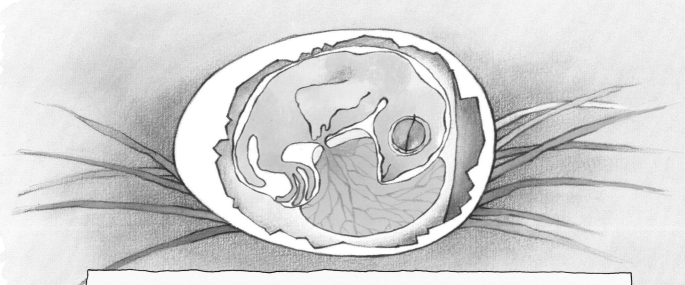

By the time the little chick is ten days old he already has wings, legs, and a beak.

By fourteen days his body is tightly curled inside the egg.

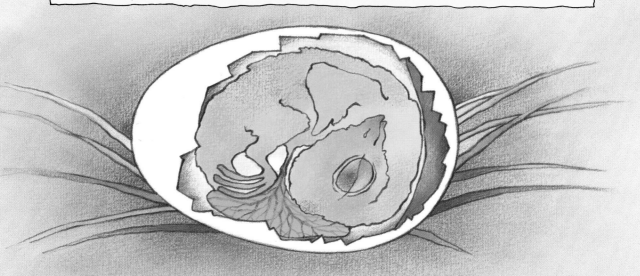

Every day the gray hen turns her eggs with her feet and her beak. This keeps the chick from sticking to the side of the shell.

Now and then the hen leaves her nest to find food.
But she hurries back before the eggs can get cold. Beginning
at the end of the third week she does not leave them at all.
The gray hen does not eat or drink. She gets very thin.

The little chick keeps growing. When all of the yolk in the egg has been taken into his body, the chick is ready to hatch. Now he is so big that he touches the shell. He can barely move. His head and body are covered with soft down. The day before he hatches, he tears a hole in the sac and breathes air from the air pocket at the end of the egg for the first time.

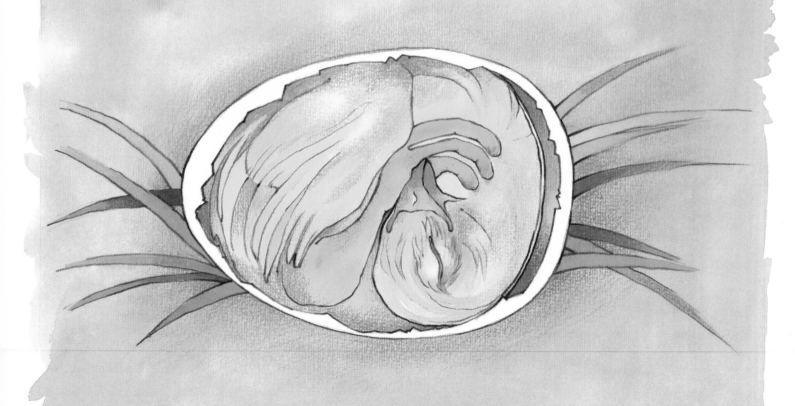

"Peep, peep," he calls from inside the egg.
"Cluck, cluck," calls back the hen.

The time has come for the chick to break out of the egg.
He uses his beak to peck a tiny opening in the shell.

Hatching is hard work. It takes about eight hours.
The chick pecks a little. Then he rests. He turns slightly
to peck some more. He pecks and then rests all day.
His legs push against the shell. Finally he pecks his
way all around the egg.

With a last stretch—*crack!*—he breaks the egg. The empty shell falls to the side and the chick tumbles out.

He is all wet and too weak to stand up.

One by one the other chicks hatch. The chicks nestle close
to the gray hen to stay warm. They all fall asleep.

By the next morning the chicks are all dry and fluffy.
They follow the gray hen in the yard. They watch her
peck for food. They peck, too.

"Cock-a-doodle-doo!" the rooster crows.

"Cheep, cheep," answer the chicks. It is a good morning on the farm.

Translation from the Spanish by Kit Maude

First English language edition published in 2022 by Tapioca Stories.
English language edition © 2022 Tapioca Stories
Originally published as *Nadadores* © 2020 Alboroto Ediciones, Mexico
Published in agreement with Phileas Fogg Agency

Library of Congress Control Number: 2021945250
ISBN: 978-1-7347839-3-3

FSC
www.fsc.org
MIX
Paper from
responsible sources
FSC® C144853

Printed in China
First Printing, 2022

TAPIOCA
STORIES

© 2022 Tapioca Stories
55 Gerard St. #455, Huntington, New York 11743
www.tapiocastories.com

TAPIOCA
STORIES

María José Ferrada

Mariana Alcántara

Swimmers

Every species has a recurring dream.

50 meters of Front Crawl

50 meters of Backstroke

50 meters of Butterfly

Fish dream of becoming
Olympic swimmers.

An unlikely dream.

A good swimmer must get
eight hours of sleep a night.

A good swimmer must have
a healthy breakfast.

A good swimmer must train every day.

And they need a suit, preferably
blue with white stripes.

It's a very unlikely dream.

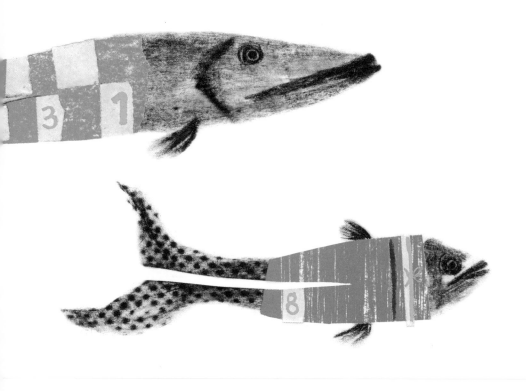

But the fish work hard every night.

Very,
very hard.

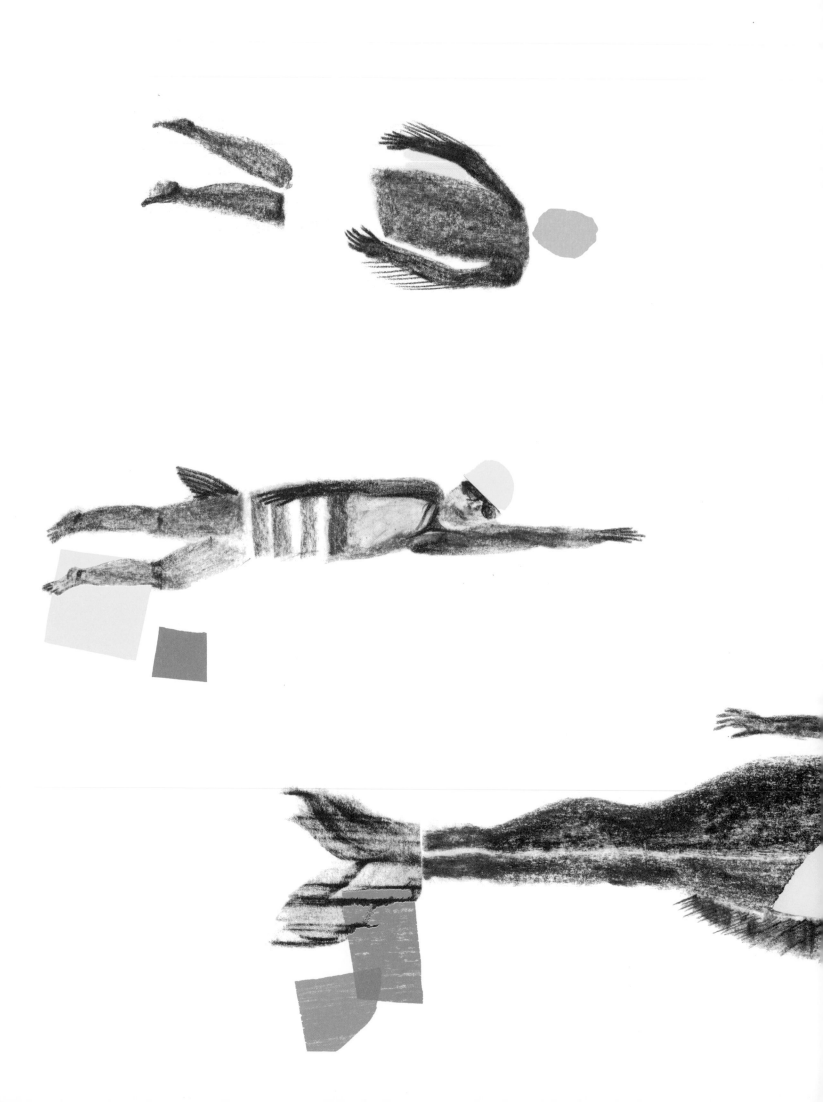

In the dream, they know that
if you want to be an Olympic swimmer,
you need to be motivated.

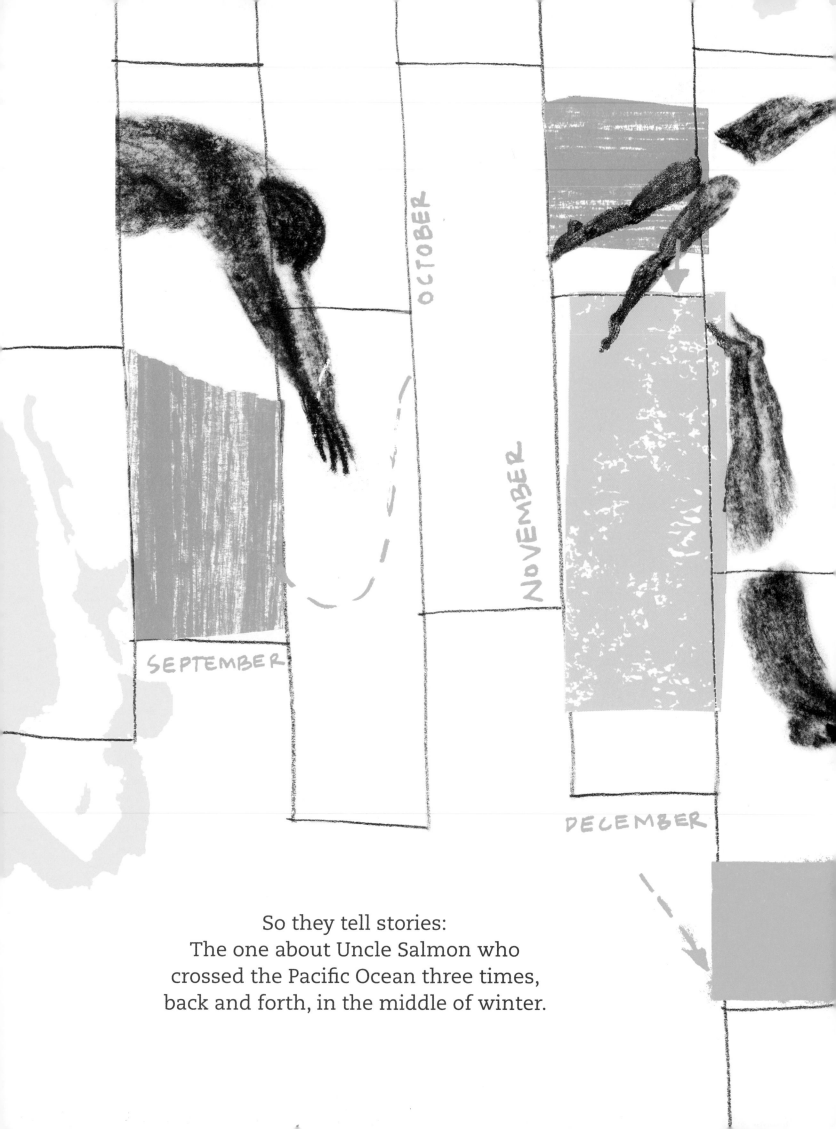

So they tell stories:
The one about Uncle Salmon who
crossed the Pacific Ocean three times,
back and forth, in the middle of winter.

APRIL

MARCH

FEBRUARY

MAY

The one about Grandma Sea Bass who only took
3 hours, 47 minutes, and 20 seconds
to swim the English Channel.

The one about the school of tuna who
won a silver medal at the 1942 Olympics.

They know the last one is made up,
but it's their favorite.

50 meters of Front Crawl

50 meters of Backstroke

50 meters of Butterfly

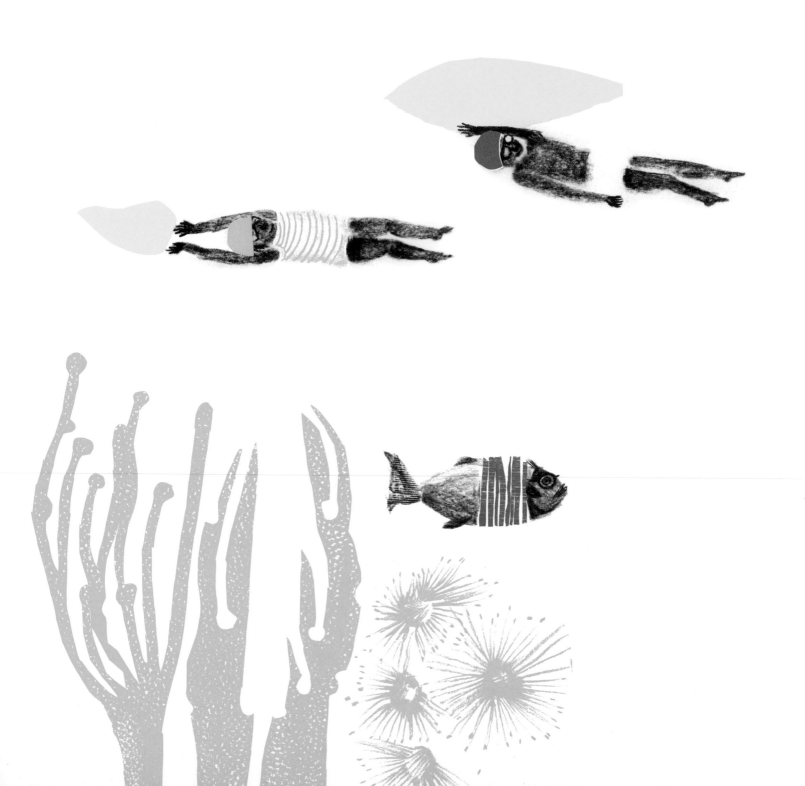

The swimmer's dream is a recurring dream
dreamed by all fish at the same time,
saltwater and freshwater alike.

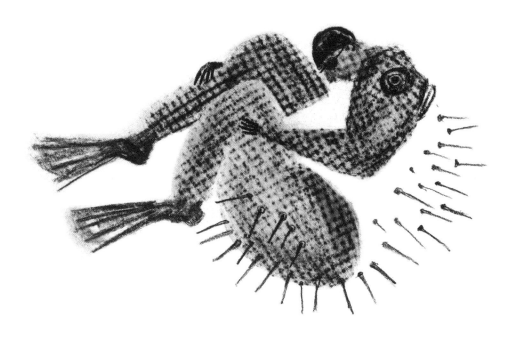

Some say it has something to do with the moon.

Others say it is the stories once told by the First Sailor.

But no one knows for sure.

The fish all wake up at the same time,
just when they've finished the
150-meter race.

Even though it's never a dream
they want to wake up from,
they aren't sad.

They know that they'll have
that dream again.

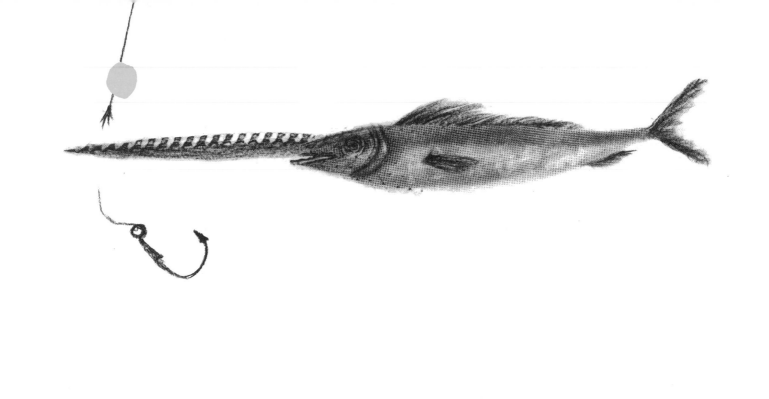

$$x^2 + 2ax + a^2$$

It's a dream that has been dreamed by fish
since the world was the world
and the sea was the sea,
and it always will be.

Remember:
all species have
a recurring dream.

50 meters of Front Crawl

50 meters of Backstroke

50 meters of Butterfly

Olympic swimmers
dream that they're fish …